HAILSTONES

Hailstones

Justin Robinson

fmsbw
San Francisco, California

ISBN 979-8-9921594-0-0

"Ascent" was first published in *Second Stutter*, Volume Three, edited by Colin Partch & Solomon Rino, 2018 (San Francisco).

Cover artwork by Michelle Fernandez Villalba

Author photo by Shannon Madrid

fmsbw

San Francisco, California

CONTENTS

FOREWORD

Justin Robinson's *Hailstones* first strikes the eye as an aural sweep of fragments implying all manner of refraction. Not a deafened stumbling of sound, but registered tremors magnified within a microscopic lingual grain. And this magnification translates in my mind to none other than psychic archery that evinces itself as sidelong penetration carrying its own velocity.

Rather than as a dazed Germanic Refugee, Robinson, rather than as a tortured member fleeing a holocaust of ghosts understands that the poetic concentration remains perpetually threatened by lemming-like mentality summoned by quotidian threat. In this sense he remains a Refugee sired by intense interior tracing, by self-protecting himself with venom sired by poetic seething. His lines, turbulent and cleansing navigating blankness via particles of explosion, via puzzling decimation, contracted, so that they attempt to enter reality as a clan of perfection.

These fragments, marked by Paul Celan, display an intensity of concision. This comparison only confers optical resemblance, in that Robinson rather than being sundered by transpersonal guilt seeks to protect his nascent germination of poetic seed from the Insidious instigation from quotidian quanta. Hailstones persists as anterior self-engenderment and exists as an extended proto-flash of many suns yet to come.

Will Alexander
San Francisco, CA

Mend

remains
the light
chair—
being
with-
out

nothing—
you reach
—climb
speak

the standing
water hand
air lifting
from the
chest—

the night
you wage
the word
rests un-
heard—

the orchid
hold—the
lake your
hand led
you—

the cloth net
time throws
endlessly a-
mending—

amethyst—
fracture the
bone you
must—

torch light
scrape the
flint mea-
sure—

palm through
water—be-
come self
separate
breath

arm green
meadow—
white silk
standing

thread crossed
artery bloom
spinal cord
the arc of
zinnia—

struck candle-
stick—carry
the ceased
root—

brain clots
come back
plums fall
the rocks
circle—

warn them
weakening
oaths pass
reach no
water—

sleep shield
coat stitch
across the
names—

nine stones
dim—you
with each
stream—

agates dot the
air you move
—stand be-
side them
once—

the psalm
near stone
blue dust
found a-
gain—

risk the parting
cloth—seam-
less—out-
ward—

three hand
color fall
what be-
gins you
have al-
ways—

Ravel

thorn each hand
together—the
windows
stand—

kneeling before
fountain—the
hexagons—
weeping
scarlet

displaced—snow
grains—remove
heart—aorta
bled stone
breath
blue

the grieving
doubles—
the white
pebbles

between us—
ground loss
this winter
glaciers
elapse

sand the arch
the twin coral
cheekbones—
toward us—
once—

flower by finger
ten crows in the
air—even here
—icepick—
comet trail
debris—

standing guard
mother skull
names fleet
the river—
two brains
swim into
them—

the minor way—
branch—ring—
sackcloth—
carry us—

stone bowl—world
water full—left
palm—frost
breathing
One—

telepath—speech
the other half
mouths un-
speaking

split comet—
pull travel far
—faced—be-
tween water
run clear—

starlings—cast
the floating rock
hand crossed—
unarmed—

levitating shoulder
—arrow in us—
strings became
the shells re-
stored—

ridge worn
light—us
—comet
crossing
spoke
again

pathless climb
the crystal
wedge—
without
touch
time

Hailstones

storm—we hand together—
this—heap of shells—
hewn—on discus—
upriver—

three candles there—
carrier—smoke sleep
home—when snow
come—water told
—stone well—
within we—

clamped shadow—
crown glow—mouth
boat—fin closer
double—speak
distance—

handprint wall—we
both—names open
worlds away from
we—cast in two
rings—

fingers ripple—
stone syllables—
Saturn—star site—
quivering voice—
splinter of ice—

skull in stream—long we
winter—hurtle forward
—flash footprint—
bitten brain—

punctured blood clot
—nine meteorites—
moons—crash
after—silk
worms—sea
stones—

wail cloth—time white
we sift—fathoms
deep—without
twin suns—

unmasked flowerbed
—cleft hand archer
whirring bow—
toward nerve
centers—

band of twigs—within
calcite cliff—cortical
ravine—pull thorns
from we—

oaths carry—first
step—arrow from
flesh—palms curl
—round cold
rocks—

child we once—kneeling
stream—shells float—
past future present—
black flower—
half mast
face—

moss on quiver—arrow
light way—when will
winter—garden
over—without
boundary—

wicker casket—clear
water rites—cloth
belt—amended
throne—rising
clay pot—

two spears—river
split—silver on
shadow—un-
sheathed—

the ram horn—
many crossing
orders—sight
near—green
withering
staff—

white jug—face
we—lost names
remain—three
fingers pelt
the star
chart

beside still water—we drop
stone knives—memory
clears—sediment—
sacrifice—mute
constellations
order the
scree

cliff back—past wood
walls—wind knots—
unravel—kinetic
reed voiced
traveler—

sun disc—split gold
speckled forehead
—bright points—
being pressed
worm white
trellis—

cleaved hands—
we've faltered—
untangle the last
walking path—

wintergreen—trench
bordered—another
rope strand—ten
cups—on card
drawn for
we—

sea roads—twin crumbling
rot beetles—we fortress
gatefold—no word
slit stone—

distant One—storm height
avow—rod spoke—fell
home—hand on chest
—held sigh—

mound—sun relation
strewn axe—quartz
wept—this side—
unnamed smoke
fire carriage—

yellow wood—oar
handed—we paddle
gap worlds—lifting
leaf—basket of
swim coins—

farer—wrist forth
a violet—two tar
ships—crag of
abandoned
shells—

frost sealed tablet
mount the breath
book—wound
ashore—be-
set there—

briar crown—abide—
forgive—rain dotted
body—founder—
ice hooved—cry
from the arms—

stray wheel—rise
from peat—still
unremembered
night—half
lost—hand
apart—

*　*　*　*　*

sand the armor plate—
pain derailing moon
—we halve
two—

render a side
overturned
mire—the
gradient
give—

lemon balm—scar signs
weave left—seer with
dagger—field sung—
where fell—hair en-
twined—

thatched hut—broken
stone lock—unarmed
across borders—we
speech each other
sound strong—

crater—torn we—parts
stick hurled—nothing
constellates—two
bark covered
shoulders
embrace
ten—

assailable shield—
glaciers return—
struck arrow—
tower wall—
grief faced—

messenger beside
twelve pentacles
comet crowned
—cut the final
fortune—

star measured—
questing axis—
clawed urchin
brine—

beyond parting levade—
wreath holder with torch
—leapt through planet
compulsion—volcanic
barnacle stones—
stood many
chiseled
free—

beacon utterance—
pierced hazel bands
—storm candle—
no crest un-
splits—

twin bowstrings
stake the desert
trough—silence
poses—fore-
sworn—silk
draped—

garment in brain—
mouth of certainty
stones—chipped
mask—fingers
breach seven
heights—

belief doubts—daylight
star—on the tables—
stammering—box
of laws—card
handed—time
conscious—
across the
water—

ice testimony—decipher
the half turned shard
carrier—throwing
silver—blank
shouldered
no sand
key—

we're still—
rock crowned
half circled—
breathing out
tomorrow's
name—

carved blade—
legends—face
breaking—be-
tween temple
gold letters
eyed—

cloth body—olive
tree—arrangement
rings—under sun
—roaming the
canticles—

to the right of
return—here
after earth—
merged with
salt—on the
square—

turned staff—un-
warred—washed
stone—shadow
—confer with
the seventh
number to-
day—

storm before we
—twin shrouds
wail—twice
the arrows
pour—

surveyor—scar
to canebrake—
four standings
in the filament
weep for both
worlds—

furious horses—
the footpath—
instar—down
the altars—
confess—

hoofs will go
—foreheads
break scroll
in song—

carved deck—
ear deep—out
step the side
stone—we
could be
grasped
again

keeled brightness
revoke the gone
blind—once
—storm—
the light
wall—

we hold root—
time—rejection
of bone—two
day steps—
unflagging
each dis-
tress—

lowland eye
centering the
ring's three
count—we
point—the
planets
face—

beneath arrows
the scale came
to promise—
the margin
of ashes
kept—

still—pilgrim—
floods carry off
the mounds on
each shoulder
—out there—
flawed uni-
verse—

redress the armor
oxhide covered
emanating left
names crush
through—
we know
them
all

Stay

moss gripped
the number
read—our
speaking
stone—

mantled grain cloth
the bawling ember
blood mouths
every crack
standing
wall—

the fortune teller
card reads one
handed script
—the keys
side—

knifed table—after
the throne—our
seedbed—the
single white
root—

mica—withstand
unlearning—our
accused—the
semblances
demand a
cypress
stick

stonecutter—
igneous—un-
certainty—
our timing
chiseled
into the
ore—

coping stone
our tree belt
ladled onto
rebellious
scales—

dovecotes
the sword
rusts—
crying
with
day

fossil crown
to sail here
tree gassed
our crutch
face—the
red be-
quest

wakened ochre
shield—there
remain—cap-
sized—the
ancestor
second
lives
out

the sandstone
ring struck—
gold flashed
a refusal—
from the
mouth

enraged hand
decontrol the
tower—our
shakable
origin

rockfalls—
field—our
names—
knelt in
court

tapped seed
the village
outskirts
stand—

heirs—grief
candles ad-
vance—lift
them up
into no-
thing

debts—twice
shell turned
the pacing
wall—

sealed—
the hand
meeting
our star
came
near

law of return
send witness
—step out
of era—

withstood quest-
ions—boulders
starred open
around our
two—

against pro-
posed reign
the keep—
recaptured
—all slain
defied—

scan the ordinance
fiercely centered
hand—through
the arrows—
our meeting
chance—

quivers flanked
left—crushing
pasture—our
sworn fled
from two
sides

persecuted
stumbled
through
gas the
table
felt—

the ridge
unearth
the half
spoken
coin—

the helmet
our watch
left brace
the three
standing
rocks—

metal chase
over birth-
rights—
among
oxen

uniforms
counter-
sign—
listing
every
name
free

the diving
branches
laboring
the arc-
hive—
under
writ
ten

our faces
front un-
to trial—
the coal
pits o-
pen

our papers
uncounted
—still the
fields—
survive
frame-
work

the knee
—speech
shared—
bright
One

rejection—
taken blind-
fold—our
reached
out—

twice be-
hind the
rope—
our for-
given
came
slant-
ing

recite our
will to the
standing
boulder
often—

names—
there the
balance
sheets
—un-
rest

reeducate
the grain
—light
stood
then

our shawl
against
faith—
wagon
down

vows—our
sea primer
—braids
pattern
shone

the shells
yellow—
fulfilled
by the
order
star

the rising
sound—
survives
the lost
count

Ascent

you—
arrows
yellow
even
now

unseat the
rule—you
hear re-
pair the
crash
altar

without arms
coat—cloth
shoulders
you this
name
day

card packed
white bark
the wheel
resolves
attains
law—

your oarlock
faith paled
earthward
cried to
sun—

undimmed
the saucer
dawning
carried
you—

daystar—
you come
recruited
it is the
first of
May

crowns shall
speak—un-
separate—
you force
pearl to
scale

let shells learn
sorrow gains
promise—
you too
soar

rights found
name—the
armbands
flashing
know
you

lips cede—
over straw
the elder
—your
tears

the court
sealed—
thinning
quest—
would
you

your gold
waves—
to fight
every
loss

you center
the candle
alliance—
hear your
second
sun

the lemon
groves—
you gain
answers
in your
mother
book

engraving
burns on
stone—
an icicle
shields
itself—
warms
itself

holding the
squares—
your exile
left from
embrace
to em-
brace

your sandal
torn—each
goat path
traveled
by you
then

strings refuse
silence—the
column will
think—the
crutched
point—
above
you

light cuts
there are
less of
you—

your leaps
handshake
the ration
script be-
longs to
you—

white song
cloth—the
demand—
your hair
grown
back

you the
reconciler
—raised in
secrecy—
the light
cycle

homeland
mistake—
origin for
honor—
your mis-
take—

the teeth
marked
coin—
this is
your
age

the comet
shimmer
there—
battles
round
you

remember
it was said
muttering
you gave
into the
gold—

you—
in the
hand
vow
you
fly

the heat
your all
pain—
where
reach
you
ran
to

you—
the last
ring—
turned
free—
turned
free

Justin Robinson, 2024

Justin Robinson was born and raised in Santa Barbara, CA. He has been teaching English Composition in San Francisco at the college and middle school levels for nine years. His poems have appeared in *Second Stutter, New American Writing, OmniVerse, F U Z Z,* and *NEW: A Biannual Journal of Contemporary American Poetry. Hailstones* is his first published book.

THE PAGE POETS SERIES

Number 12
The Public Sound by Marina Lazzara

Number 13
Record of Records by Rod Roland

Number 14
Strangers We Have Known by John Briscoe

Number 15
Cutting Teeth by Jesse Holwitz

Number 16
Other Scavengers by Lauren Caldwell

Number 17
Cueonia by Jesse Holwitz

Number 18
In the Museum of Hunting and Nature by Cynthia Randolph

Number 19
A New Species of Color by Tamsin Spencer Smith

Number 20
Busy Secret by Micah Ballard

Number 21
Out of the Blue by Fran Carbonaro

Number 22
Broadway Azaleas by Sunnylyn Thibodeaux

Number 23
War News II by Beau Beausoleil

Number 24
Hailstones by Justin Robinson

www.ingramcontent.com/pod-product-compliance
Lightning Source LLC
Chambersburg PA
CBHW032046040426
42449CB00007B/1002